By the skin
of my
chinny chin chin

"I spy with my little eye,"
said the ugly old fox,
"a plump little pig."

2

"I am very hungry,"
puffed the ugly old fox,

"and when I am very hungry
I like to eat plump little pigs."

"Come out, little pig,
come out and play,"
said the ugly old fox.

"I love little pigs.
I love plump little pigs a lot!
Please come out and play with me."

"Oh no! No, no, no!"
said the little pig.
"By the skin of my chinny chin chin,
I will not play with you.
You will eat me.
Go away you ugly old fox."

"Grrrrr..." went the ugly old fox.
"Then I'll huff, and I'll puff and
I'll blow your house down."

So the ugly old fox huffed and he
puffed and he blew the house down!

"Help! Help! Help!" yelled the little
pig, and he ran to the house of the
middle-size pig.

"I spy with my little eye,"
said the ugly old fox,
"a plump middle-size pig.
Come out, middle-size pig,
come out and play,"
said the ugly old fox.

"I love middle-size pigs.
I love plump middle-size pigs a lot!
Please come out and play with me."

"Oh no! No, no, no!"
said the middle-size pig.
"By the skin of my chinny chin chin,
I will not play with you.
You will eat me.
Go away you ugly old fox."

"Grrrrr...," went the ugly old fox.
"Then I'll huff, and I'll puff and
I'll blow your house down."

The ugly old fox huffed and he
puffed and he blew the house down!

"Help! Help! Help!" yelled
the two pigs, and they ran to
the house of the big pig.

"I spy with my little eye,"
said the ugly old fox,
"a plump big pig."

"Come out, big pig, come out and
play," said the ugly old fox.
"I love big pigs.
I love plump big pigs a lot!
Please come out and play with me."

"Oh no! No, no, no!"
said the plump big pig.
"By the skin of my chinny chin chin,
I will not play with you.
You will eat me.
Go away you ugly old fox."

"Grrrrr...," went the ugly old fox.
"Then I'll huff, and I'll puff and
I'll blow your house down."

The ugly old fox huffed
and he puffed and ...

he huffed and he puffed ...

but the house did not fall down!

"I will get you!" yelled the cross
old fox. "I will, I will, I will!"

"I've got a plan," said the big pig.
"By the skin of my chinny chin chin,
I will make that old fox run away.

I will make him run and run and run."

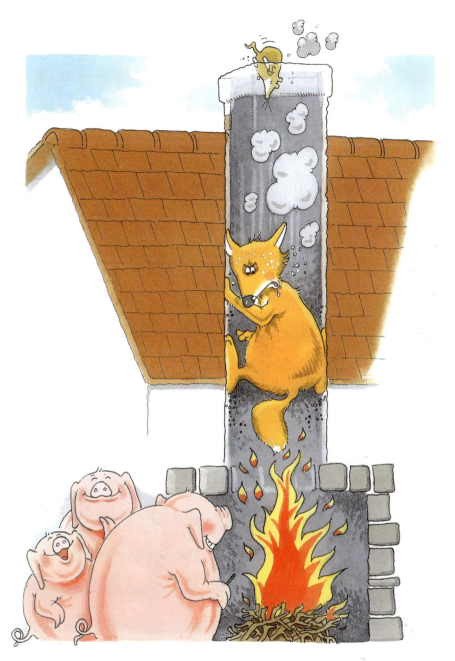

So, just as the old fox came down…